THE
ITALY
TRAVEL JOURNAL

FOR DOCUMENTING YOUR
ADVENTURES IN ITALY

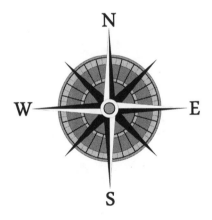

YOUNGHUSBAND
WORLD TRAVEL JOURNALS™

ABOUT

THIS TRAVEL JOURNAL IS OWNED BY

IF THIS JOURNAL IS LOST, PLEASE BE SO KIND AS TO RETURN IT TO / CONTACT

STARTED

FINISHED

ALDOUS HUXLEY

FOR EVERY TRAVELLER WHO HAS ANY TASTE OF HIS OWN, THE ONLY USEFUL GUIDEBOOK WILL BE THE ONE WHICH HE HIMSELF HAS WRITTEN

HOW TO USE THIS TRAVEL JOURNAL

THE ITALY TRAVEL JOURNAL has been carefully crafted by the legendary designer and nomad Cormac Younghusband to help make your trip unforgettable, fun and organized—with plenty of room for spontaneity and new discoveries too. This journal can help you plan, live out and record every stage of your journey to Italy—from pre-trip, to getting there, to being there, to getting home, and afterwards.

ABOUT. This is a place to record who the journal belongs to and contact information in case of loss. There's a spot to record when you started writing in the journal and when you finished.

IMPORTANT INFORMATION. When you travel to Italy, you will want to make note here of important contact information, important documents details, flight numbers, car rental info, hotel bookings, emergency numbers, and the like.

COUNTRY BRIEF + MAP. Read up on Italy. The Country Brief contains the following sections: Introduction, Geography, Demographics, National Notes, Economy, Internet & Communications, and advice for travelers. There's a map of Italy at the end of the brief.

INSPIRATION. What has inspired you to take this trip? Was your inspiration literary, a film, television, the Internet, word-of-mouth, family, business, sport? When the trip is over, what do you want to be able to say about it? What will make this journey to Italy a success?

ABOUT MY JOURNEY. Write about the who, what, where, when and how of the trip you are planning. Make special note of when you depart home, return home, and your budget.

TRAVEL COMPANIONS. Traveling alone can be wonderful, but more often than not we travel with companions. Who are you traveling with? Jot their names and numbers here.

RESEARCH. Before you go, do your research. Read the relevant Italy travel guides and websites. Take notes on: places to go / explore, places to stay, places to shop / must have souvenirs, cultural / sporting events to attend, historical / religious sites of interest, pubs-bars-places-to-party, beaches / forests / natural wonders to see, parks & gardens to wander through, things to eat and drink / dining experiences, festivals & events to attend, stuff for kids - seniors - and such, experiences to experience, important local customs, etiquette and laws. There is also room for research on other stuff you are interested in. It often yields dividends to research important words and phrases in the local language.

ITINERARY. Make an itinerary to schedule all the stuff you want to do. Write out when and where/what you want to do. An itinerary is a plan. You do not have to stick to it, unless you want to. Check off the itinerary items as you complete them.

JOURNEY CHECKLIST. There's lots to do when taking trips. Write down all of your to-do items and then check them off as you get them done.

GETTING THERE. Some folks say that the journey is more important than the destination. Lots can happen on the way. Tell your story of getting there.

ARRIVAL. You have arrived in Italy! Where did you enter the country? When did you arrive? By what mode of transportation did you arrive? What was your arrival like? Use this page to take a few notes on this momentous event.

BEING THERE. You are in Italy. First impressions? What are your thoughts and feelings? What are the sights and sounds that most impressed you?

STUFF BOUGHT / SOUVENIRS. Keep track of the stuff you buy, what it cost in the local currency and what it costs in your home currency..

PEOPLE MET ALONG THE WAY. One of the great joys of travel is meeting new and interesting people from all over the world. Keep in touch with those you meet by jotting down their names and contact information here.

DAILY RECORDS. In the daily records, there is space to capture your travel memories. There are enough entries for fifty days. The Daily Record journal fields are:

DAY #. What day of your journey is this?

DATE. What's the date?

WIND/RAIN/ SKY. What was the day like? How windy? Did it rain? Was the sky blue and clear, overcast, storm clouds?

TEMP. What's the temperature today?

LOCATION(S). Jot down a summary of all the places visited today.

WHAT HAPPENED TODAY + THOUGHS ON WHAT HAPPENED. Jot down a simple account of the day's events, for example: dates and times; encounters; details of excursion; arrival at the airport; the interesting banter of the tattooed gentlemen; the taxi driver's travel tips; the name of the hotel; your whimsical discovery; et cetera. Document your thoughts about what happened: what memories did the events evoke; what ideas occurred to you in response to your encounters?

HIGHLIGHT OF THE DAY. For better or for worse, what was the single most noteworthy event today?

NOTES. Use this section to write about anything you want. Next to the note section is a great list of subjects to help you decide on what to write about. Or, use this space to make a map or sketch or doodle.

DEPARTURE. Ready or not, the time has come to leave! Where did you depart Italy from? When did you depart? What mode of transportation did you use to make your exit? What was your departure like? What happened? How were you feeling? Use this page to take a few notes on this momentous event and on getting home.

HIGHLIGHT LISTS. List out the highlights of your trip!

COUNTRY RADAR. Use the Country Radar to create a signature review of your visit to Italy. Fill in the radar blips (dots) for each review dimension (and add two of your own). There are four levels for each dimension: excellent, good, fair, and terrible. The blip closest to the outer edge is excellent and closest to the center is terrible. When all the blips are filled in, connect them with a line and shade in the area—the larger the shaded area, the more you liked the country. The result is your own unique signature radar pattern reflecting your overall impression of your journey to Italy. Use this to weigh the good and the bad and clarify your feelings and impressions.

○ EXCELLENT

○ GOOD

○ FAIR

○ TERRIBLE

CLIMATE / WEATHER. What did you think about the climate?

SCENERY / SIGHTS. What impressions did you have of the scenery / sights of Italy?

UNPOLLUTED ENVIRONMENT. Did you find the country clean and fresh or dirty and polluted?

B L A N K (YOU FILL THIS ONE IN). You decide what this one measures. What are you interested in? Golf? Churches? National dance?

FRIENDLINESS / GROSS NATIONAL HAPPINESS. Were the locals friendly? Happy? Or, not so much?

FOOD & DRINK. What did you think of the national food and drink in Italy?

CULTURAL OPPORTUNITIES. Rate you experience with Italy's cultural opportunities?

ADVENTURE OPPORTUNITIES. Rate you experience with Italy's adventure opportunities?

REST & RELAXATION OPPORTUNITIES. Rate you experience with Italy's rest and relaxation opportunities?

INTERESTING / FUN (NOT BORING). Did you find Italy interesting and fun? As opposed to boring and dull?

ACCOMMODATIONS. How did you find the places you stayed? Were they up to your standards?

TRANSPORTATION. What did you think of the transportation you took inside the country? Was getting around a piece of cake or slice of hell?

COST-OF-LIVING / AFFORDABILITY. How did you find the cost-of-living in Italy? Was it an affordable destination for you?

SAFETY. Was it safe in Italy?

B L A N K (YOU FILL THIS ONE IN). You decide what this one measures. What are you interested in? Beaches? Surf? Beer? Museums? Chocolate?

RE-VISIT WORTHINESS. Is Italy re-visit worthy? Do you wish you were there now? Or, are you delighted to have shaken off the dust of this country?

COUNTRY REVIEW & RATING. Write a review of the country and give it a no-star to five star rating.

AFTERWARDS. You are home. You've had a chance to reflect on your time spent traveling in Italy. Sum up the story of your journey here.

TRAVEL WISH LIST. When one journey ends, start planning the next! Here is a spot to start thinking about where you would like to go next.

GENERIC PACKING IDEAS. Use the Younghusband Packing System to help you make sure your packing is as complete as possible.

MEASURES & THEIR CONVERSIONS. For your ease of reference, this section sets out some standard and metric measures and their conversions.

NOTES, SKETCHES, MAPS. Here's a place for grid, lined, and blank notes, sketches, and map-making.

IMPORTANT INFORMATION
PEOPLE :: CONTACT INFO ::: DOCUMENTS + DETAILS

ITALY

TIME ZONE: *UTC+1*
POPULATION: *61,261,254*

INTRODUCTION

Italy is a republic. The country is located at 42 50 N, 12 50 E.

Italy became a nation-state in 1861 when the regional states of the peninsula, along with Sardinia and Sicily, were united under King Victor EMMANUEL II. An era of parliamentary government came to a close in the early 1920s when Benito MUSSOLINI established a Fascist dictatorship. His alliance with Nazi Germany led to Italy's defeat in World War II. A democratic republic replaced the monarchy in 1946 and economic revival followed. Italy is a charter member of NATO and the European Economic Community (EEC). It has been at the forefront of European economic and political unification, joining the Economic and Monetary Union in 1999. Persistent problems include sluggish economic growth, low youth and female employment, organized crime, corruption, and economic disparities between southern Italy and the more prosperous north.

GEOGRAPHY

The capital of Italy is Rome and it is located at 41 54 N, 12 29 E.

The primary administrative regions of the country are: 15 regions (regioni, singular - regione) and 5 autonomous regions (regioni autonome, singular - regione autonoma).

The total area of the country is 301,340 sq km.

The country's climate is: predominantly Mediterranean; Alpine in far north; hot, dry in south. Natural hazards include: regional risks include landslides, mudflows, avalanches, earthquakes, volcanic eruptions, flooding; land subsidence in Venice ; volcanism: significant volcanic activity; Etna (elev. 3,330 m), which is in eruption as of 2010, is Europe's most active volcano; flank eruptions pose a threat to nearby Sicilian villages; Etna, along with the famous Vesuvius, which remains a threat to the millions of nearby residents in the Bay of Naples area, have both been deemed "Decade Volcanoes" by the International Association of Volcanology and Chemistry of the Earth's Interior, worthy of study due to their explosive history and close proximity to human populations; Stromboli, on its namesake island, has also been continuously active with moderate volcanic activity; other historically active volcanoes include Campi Flegrei, Ischia, Larderello, Pantelleria, Vulcano, and Vulsini. It has mostly rugged and mountainous; some plains, coastal lowlands.

The primary natural resources of Italy are: coal, mercury, zinc, potash, marble, barite, asbestos, pumice, fluorspar, feldspar, pyrite (sulfur), natural gas and crude oil reserves, fish, arable land. Italy is 26.41% arable land and the amount of land devoted to permanent agriculture is 9.09%. The portion of land devoted other uses is 64.5% (2005).

It's total land area is 294,140 sq km and total water resources are 7,200 sq km. The country has 7,600 km of coastline. The lowest point in the country is: Mediterranean Sea 0 m. The highest point in the country is: Mont Blanc (Monte Bianco) de Courmayeur 4,748 m (a secondary peak of Mont Blanc).

Some of the environment challenges faced by Italy include: air pollution from industrial emissions such as sulfur dioxide; coastal and inland rivers polluted from industrial and agricultural effluents; acid rain damaging lakes; inadequate industrial waste treatment and disposal facilities.

Of geographic interest: strategic location dominating central Mediterranean as well as southern sea and air approaches to Western Europe.

DEMOGRAPHICS

The population of Italy ranks 23 out of the approximately 242 countries and territories of the world.

The 61,261,254 inhabitants of Italy are: Italian (includes small clusters of German-, French-, and Slovene-Italians in the north and Albanian-Italians and Greek-Italians in the south).

The primary languages spoken are: Italian (official), German (parts of Trentino-Alto Adige region are predominantly German speaking), French (small French-speaking minority in Valle d'Aosta region), Slovene (Slovene-speaking minority in the Trieste-Gorizia area).

The religious make-up of Italy is: Christian 80% (overwhelming Roman Catholic with very small groups of Jehova Witnesses and Protestants), Muslims NEGL (about 700,000 but growing), Atheists and Agnostics 20%.

NATIONAL NOTES

Independence came for Italy on 17 March 1861 (Kingdom of Italy proclaimed; Italy was not finally unified until 1870).

It's national day is: Republic Day, 2 June (1946).

The white, five-pointed star (Stella d'Italia) is the national symbol. The country's flag consists of three equal vertical bands of green (hoist side), white, and red; design inspired by the French flag brought to Italy by Napoleon in 1797; colors are those of Milan (red and white) combined with the green uniform color of the Milanese civic guard.

Italy spends 1.8% of its GDP on its military. This spending ranks Italy 82 out of the approximately 242 countries and territories of the world.

ECONOMY

Italy's GDP in US Dollars is $1.98 trillion (2012 est.) and it's primary trading partners are: Germany 16.5%, France 8.8%, China 7.7%, Netherlands 5.5%, Spain 4.7% (2011).

Italy's agricultural production consists of: fruits, vegetables, grapes, potatoes, sugar beets, soybeans, grain, olives; beef, dairy products; fish.

The primary industries are: tourism, machinery, iron and steel, chemicals, food processing, textiles, motor vehicles, clothing, footwear, ceramics.

They key exports of Italy are: engineering products, textiles and clothing, production machinery, motor vehicles, transport equipment, chemicals; food, beverages and tobacco; minerals, and nonferrous metals.

The primary imports are: engineering products, chemicals, transport equipment, energy products, minerals and nonferrous metals, textiles and clothing; food, beverages, and tobacco.

Italy has a diversified industrial economy, which is divided into a developed industrial north, dominated by private companies, and a less-developed, highly subsidized, agricultural south, with high unemployment. The Italian economy is driven in large part by the manufacture of high-quality consumer goods produced by small and medium-sized enterprises, many of them family owned. Italy also has a sizable underground economy, which by some estimates accounts for as much as 17% of GDP. These activities are most common within the agriculture, construction, and service sectors. Italy is the third-largest economy in the euro-zone, but its exceptionally high public debt and structural impediments to growth have rendered it vulnerable to scrutiny by financial markets. Public debt has increased steadily since 2007, topping 126% of GDP in 2012, and investor concerns about the broader euro-zone crisis at times have caused borrowing costs on sovereign government debt to rise to euro-era records. During the second half of 2011 the government passed a series of three austerity packages to balance its budget and decrease its public debt. These measures included a hike in the value-added tax, pension reforms, and cuts to public administration. The government also faces pressure from investors and European partners to sustain its recent efforts to address Italy's long-standing structural impediments to growth, such as an inflexible labor market and widespread tax evasion. In 2012 economic growth and labor market conditions deteriorated, with growth at -2.3% and unemployment rising to nearly 11%. Although the government has undertaken several economic reform iniatiatives, in the longer-term Italy's low fertility rate, productivity, and foreign investment will increasingly strain its economy. Italy's GDP is now 7% below its 2007 pre-crisis level.

INTERNET & COMMUNICATIONS

29.235 million (2009) of Italy's 61,261,254 citizens are Internet users. The country's Internet country code is: .it

The dialling code for Italy is: 39.

Communications infrastructure assessment: high-capacity cable and microwave radio relay trunks.

ADVICE ON TRAVELING TO ITALY

The health and safety conditions of any country have the potential to change quickly. No matter where in the world you intend to travel, make sure you check with your Government for travel advice, warnings or advisories. Review this information while planning your trip and shortly before undertaking your trip. The decision to travel is always the sole responsibility of the individual.

MAP OF ITALY

INSPIRATION

ABOUT MY JOURNEY

DEPART	RETURN	BUDGET

TRAVEL COMPANIONS
NAME + INFO

RESEARCH

PLACES TO GO / EXPLORE

PLACES TO STAY

PLACES TO SHOP / MUST HAVE SOUVENIRS

RESEARCH

CULTURAL / SPORTING EVENTS TO ATTEND

HISTORICAL / RELIGIOUS SITES OF INTEREST

PUBS / BARS / PLACES TO PARTy

RESEARCH

FESTIVALS & EVENTS TO ATTEND

STUFF FOR KIDS, SENIORS, AND SUCH

EXPERIENCES TO EXPERIENCE

RESEARCH

BEACHES / FORESTS / NATURAL WONDERS TO SEE

PARKS & GARDENS TO WANDER THROUGH

THINGS TO EAT & DRINK / DINING EXPERIENCES

RESEARCH

IMPORTANT LOCAL CUSTOMS, ETIQUETTE, LAWS

RESEARCH

RESEARCH
IMPORTANT WORDS & PHRASES IN THE LOCAL LANGUAGE(S)

LOCAL

TRANSLATION

LOCAL

TRANSLATION

LOCAL

TRANSLATION

LOCAL

TRANSLATION

LOCAL

TRANSLATION

LOCAL

TRANSLATION

LOCAL

TRANSLATION

LOCAL

TRANSLATION

LOCAL

TRANSLATION

LOCAL

TRANSLATION

LOCAL

TRANSLATION

LOCAL

TRANSLATION

LOCAL

TRANSLATION

LOCAL

TRANSLATION

ITINERARY

WHEN + WHERE + CHECK IT WHEN YOU'VE DONE IT

- [ ]
- [ ]
- [ ]
- [ ]
- [ ]
- [ ]
- [ ]
- [ ]
- [ ]
- [ ]
- [ ]
- [ ]
- [ ]
- [ ]
- [ ]
- [ ]
- [ ]
- [ ]
- [ ]
- [ ]
- [ ]
- [ ]
- [ ]

ITINERARY

WHEN + WHERE + CHECK IT WHEN YOU'VE DONE IT

- [ ]
- [ ]
- [ ]
- [ ]
- [ ]
- [ ]
- [ ]
- [ ]
- [ ]
- [ ]
- [ ]
- [ ]
- [ ]
- [ ]
- [ ]
- [ ]
- [ ]
- [ ]
- [ ]
- [ ]
- [ ]

JOURNEY CHECKLIST

WHEN + WHERE + CHECK IT WHEN YOU'VE DONE IT

JOURNEY CHECKLIST

WHEN + WHERE + CHECK IT WHEN YOU'VE DONE IT

- [ ]
- [ ]
- [ ]
- [ ]
- [ ]
- [ ]
- [ ]
- [ ]
- [ ]
- [ ]
- [ ]
- [ ]
- [ ]
- [ ]
- [ ]
- [ ]
- [ ]
- [ ]
- [ ]
- [ ]
- [ ]
- [ ]

JOSEPH CONRAD

GOING UP THAT RIVER WAS LIKE TRAVELLING BACK TO THE EARLIEST BEGINNINGS OF THE WORLD, WHEN VEGETATION RIOTED ON THE EARTH AND THE BIG TREES WERE KINGS.

ARRIVAL

ARRIVED WHERE	ARRIVED WHEN	ARRIVED BY

ARRIVAL NOTES

STUFF BOUGHT / SOUVENIRS
THING + LOCAL PRICE + HOME PRICE

STUFF BOUGHT / SOUVENIRS

THING + LOCAL PRICE + HOME PRICE

MY DREAM IS TO WALK AROUND THE WORLD. A SMALLISH BACKPACK, ALL ESSENTIALS NEATLY IN PLACE. A CAMERA. A NOTEBOOK....

PEOPLE MET ALONG THE WAY

NAME + INFO

DAY #	DATE	WIND / RAIN / SKY	TEMP

LOCATION(S)

WHAT HAPPENED TODAY + THOUGHTS ON WHAT HAPPENED

HIGHLIGHT OF THE DAY

NOTES

DAY #	DATE	WIND / RAIN / SKY	TEMP

LOCATION(S)

WHAT HAPPENED TODAY + THOUGHTS ON WHAT HAPPENED

HIGHLIGHT OF THE DAY

NOTES

DAY #	DATE	WIND / RAIN / SKY	TEMP

LOCATION(S)

WHAT HAPPENED TODAY + THOUGHTS ON WHAT HAPPENED

HIGHLIGHT OF THE DAY

ACCOMMODATIONS
ADVENTURE
ART
AVOID+THIS
BARS
BEACHES
BELIEFS
BEST+THING
BEVERAGES
BOOKS
BOUGHT
CHURCHES
CLIMATE
CONVERSATION
CUSTOMS
DREAMS
ENCOUNTERS
EVENTS
EXHIBITIONS
EXPENSES
EXPERIENCES
FESTIVALS
FLORA+FAUNA
FOOD
GALLERIES
GARDENS
GEOGRAPHY
GETTING AROUND
HANDICRAFTS
HEALTH
HISTORY
HOLIDAYS
HOTEL
IDEAS
LANDMARKS
LANGUAGE
LEGENDS
MARKET
MEALS
MEDIA
MEMORIES
MONEY
MOVIES
MUSEUMS
MUSIC
NAMES+FACES
NATIONAL+PARKS
NATURE
NIGHT LIFE
PARKS
POLITICS
RECIPES
RESTAURANTS
SAFETY
SHOPPING
SMELLS
SOUNDS
SOUVENIRS
SPORT
STORIES
TEMPLES
THOUGHTS
TOURS
USEFUL+PHRASES
TRANSPORTATION
WARNINGS
WEATHER
WILDLIFE
WORST+THING

NOTES

DAY #	DATE	WIND / RAIN / SKY	TEMP

LOCATION(S)

WHAT HAPPENED TODAY + THOUGHTS ON WHAT HAPPENED

HIGHLIGHT OF THE DAY

NOTES

DAY #	DATE	WIND / RAIN / SKY	TEMP

LOCATION(S)

WHAT HAPPENED TODAY + THOUGHTS ON WHAT HAPPENED

HIGHLIGHT OF THE DAY

NOTES

DAY #	DATE	WIND / RAIN / SKY	TEMP

LOCATION(S)

WHAT HAPPENED TODAY + THOUGHTS ON WHAT HAPPENED

HIGHLIGHT OF THE DAY

NOTES

DAY #	DATE	WIND / RAIN / SKY	TEMP

LOCATION(S)

WHAT HAPPENED TODAY + THOUGHTS ON WHAT HAPPENED

HIGHLIGHT OF THE DAY

NOTES

DAY #	DATE	WIND / RAIN / SKY	TEMP

LOCATION(S)

WHAT HAPPENED TODAY + THOUGHTS ON WHAT HAPPENED

HIGHLIGHT OF THE DAY

NOTES

DAY #	DATE	WIND / RAIN / SKY	TEMP

LOCATION(S)

WHAT HAPPENED TODAY + THOUGHTS ON WHAT HAPPENED

HIGHLIGHT OF THE DAY

ACCOMMODATIONS
ADVENTURE
ART
AVOID+THIS
BARS
BEACHES
BELIEFS
BEST+THING
BEVERAGES
BOOKS
BOUGHT
CHURCHES
CLIMATE
CONVERSATION
CUSTOMS
DREAMS
ENCOUNTERS
EVENTS
EXHIBITIONS
EXPENSES
EXPERIENCES
FESTIVALS
FLORA+FAUNA
FOOD
GALLERIES
GARDENS
GEOGRAPHY
GETTING AROUND
HANDICRAFTS
HEALTH
HISTORY
HOLIDAYS
HOTEL
IDEAS
LANDMARKS
LANGUAGE
LEGENDS
MARKET
MEALS
MEDIA
MEMORIES
MONEY
MOVIES
MUSEUMS
MUSIC
NAMES+FACES
NATIONAL+PARKS
NATURE
NIGHT LIFE
PARKS
POLITICS
RECIPES
RESTAURANTS
SAFETY
SHOPPING
SMELLS
SOUNDS
SOUVENIRS
SPORT
STORIES
TEMPLES
THOUGHTS
TOURS
USEFUL+PHRASES
TRANSPORTATION
WARNINGS
WEATHER
WILDLIFE
WORST+THING

NOTES

| DAY # | DATE | WIND / RAIN / SKY | TEMP |

LOCATION(S)

WHAT HAPPENED TODAY + THOUGHTS ON WHAT HAPPENED

HIGHLIGHT OF THE DAY

NOTES

DAY #	DATE	WIND / RAIN / SKY	TEMP

LOCATION(S)

WHAT HAPPENED TODAY + THOUGHTS ON WHAT HAPPENED

HIGHLIGHT OF THE DAY

NOTES

DAY #	DATE	WIND / RAIN / SKY	TEMP

LOCATION(S)

WHAT HAPPENED TODAY + THOUGHTS ON WHAT HAPPENED

HIGHLIGHT OF THE DAY

NOTES

DAY #	DATE	WIND / RAIN / SKY	TEMP

LOCATION(S)

WHAT HAPPENED TODAY + THOUGHTS ON WHAT HAPPENED

HIGHLIGHT OF THE DAY

NOTES

DAY #	DATE	WIND / RAIN / SKY	TEMP

LOCATION(S)

WHAT HAPPENED TODAY + THOUGHTS ON WHAT HAPPENED

HIGHLIGHT OF THE DAY

NOTES

DAY #	DATE	WIND / RAIN / SKY	TEMP

LOCATION(S)

WHAT HAPPENED TODAY + THOUGHTS ON WHAT HAPPENED

HIGHLIGHT OF THE DAY

NOTES

DAY #	DATE	WIND / RAIN / SKY	TEMP

LOCATION(S)

WHAT HAPPENED TODAY + THOUGHTS ON WHAT HAPPENED

HIGHLIGHT OF THE DAY

NOTES

DAY #	DATE	WIND / RAIN / SKY	TEMP

LOCATION(S)

WHAT HAPPENED TODAY + THOUGHTS ON WHAT HAPPENED

HIGHLIGHT OF THE DAY

ACCOMMODATIONS
ADVENTURE
ART
AVOID+THIS
BARS
BEACHES
BELIEFS
BEST+THING
BEVERAGES
BOOKS
BOUGHT
CHURCHES
CLIMATE
CONVERSATION
CUSTOMS
DREAMS
ENCOUNTERS
EVENTS
EXHIBITIONS
EXPENSES
EXPERIENCES
FESTIVALS
FLORA+FAUNA
FOOD
GALLERIES
GARDENS
GEOGRAPHY
GETTING AROUND
HANDICRAFTS
HEALTH
HISTORY
HOLIDAYS
HOTEL
IDEAS
LANDMARKS
LANGUAGE
LEGENDS
MARKET
MEALS
MEDIA
MEMORIES
MONEY
MOVIES
MUSEUMS
MUSIC
NAMES+FACES
NATIONAL+PARKS
NATURE
NIGHT LIFE
PARKS
POLITICS
RECIPES
RESTAURANTS
SAFETY
SHOPPING
SMELLS
SOUNDS
SOUVENIRS
SPORT
STORIES
TEMPLES
THOUGHTS
TOURS
USEFUL+PHRASES
TRANSPORTATION
WARNINGS
WEATHER
WILDLIFE
WORST+THING

NOTES

DAY #	DATE	WIND / RAIN / SKY	TEMP

LOCATION(S)

WHAT HAPPENED TODAY + THOUGHTS ON WHAT HAPPENED

HIGHLIGHT OF THE DAY

NOTES

DAY #	DATE	WIND / RAIN / SKY	TEMP

LOCATION(S)

WHAT HAPPENED TODAY + THOUGHTS ON WHAT HAPPENED

HIGHLIGHT OF THE DAY

NOTES

DAY #	DATE	WIND / RAIN / SKY	TEMP

LOCATION(S)

WHAT HAPPENED TODAY + THOUGHTS ON WHAT HAPPENED

HIGHLIGHT OF THE DAY

NOTES

DAY #	DATE	WIND / RAIN / SKY	TEMP

LOCATION(S)

WHAT HAPPENED TODAY + THOUGHTS ON WHAT HAPPENED

HIGHLIGHT OF THE DAY

NOTES

DAY #	DATE	WIND / RAIN / SKY	TEMP

LOCATION(S)

WHAT HAPPENED TODAY + THOUGHTS ON WHAT HAPPENED

HIGHLIGHT OF THE DAY

NOTES

DAY #	DATE	WIND / RAIN / SKY	TEMP

LOCATION(S)

WHAT HAPPENED TODAY + THOUGHTS ON WHAT HAPPENED

HIGHLIGHT OF THE DAY

NOTES

DAY #	DATE	WIND / RAIN / SKY	TEMP

LOCATION(S)

WHAT HAPPENED TODAY + THOUGHTS ON WHAT HAPPENED

HIGHLIGHT OF THE DAY

NOTES

DAY #	DATE	WIND / RAIN / SKY	TEMP

LOCATION(S)

WHAT HAPPENED TODAY + THOUGHTS ON WHAT HAPPENED

HIGHLIGHT OF THE DAY

NOTES

DAY #	DATE	WIND / RAIN / SKY	TEMP

LOCATION(S)

WHAT HAPPENED TODAY + THOUGHTS ON WHAT HAPPENED

HIGHLIGHT OF THE DAY

NOTES

DAY #	DATE	WIND / RAIN / SKY	TEMP

LOCATION(S)

WHAT HAPPENED TODAY + THOUGHTS ON WHAT HAPPENED

HIGHLIGHT OF THE DAY

NOTES

DAY #	DATE	WIND / RAIN / SKY	TEMP

LOCATION(S)

WHAT HAPPENED TODAY + THOUGHTS ON WHAT HAPPENED

HIGHLIGHT OF THE DAY

NOTES

DAY #	DATE	WIND / RAIN / SKY	TEMP

LOCATION(S)

WHAT HAPPENED TODAY + THOUGHTS ON WHAT HAPPENED

HIGHLIGHT OF THE DAY

NOTES

DAY #	DATE	WIND / RAIN / SKY	TEMP

LOCATION(S)

WHAT HAPPENED TODAY + THOUGHTS ON WHAT HAPPENED

HIGHLIGHT OF THE DAY

NOTES

DAY #	DATE	WIND / RAIN / SKY	TEMP

LOCATION(S)

WHAT HAPPENED TODAY + THOUGHTS ON WHAT HAPPENED

HIGHLIGHT OF THE DAY

NOTES

DAY #	DATE	WIND / RAIN / SKY	TEMP

LOCATION(S)

WHAT HAPPENED TODAY + THOUGHTS ON WHAT HAPPENED

HIGHLIGHT OF THE DAY

NOTES

DAY #	DATE	WIND / RAIN / SKY	TEMP

LOCATION(S)

WHAT HAPPENED TODAY + THOUGHTS ON WHAT HAPPENED

HIGHLIGHT OF THE DAY

ACCOMMODATIONS
ADVENTURE
ART
AVOID+THIS
BARS
BEACHES
BELIEFS
BEST+THING
BEVERAGES
BOOKS
BOUGHT
CHURCHES
CLIMATE
CONVERSATION
CUSTOMS
DREAMS
ENCOUNTERS
EVENTS
EXHIBITIONS
EXPENSES
EXPERIENCES
FESTIVALS
FLORA+FAUNA
FOOD
GALLERIES
GARDENS
GEOGRAPHY
GETTING AROUND
HANDICRAFTS
HEALTH
HISTORY
HOLIDAYS
HOTEL
IDEAS
LANDMARKS
LANGUAGE
LEGENDS
MARKET
MEALS
MEDIA
MEMORIES
MONEY
MOVIES
MUSEUMS
MUSIC
NAMES+FACES
NATIONAL+PARKS
NATURE
NIGHT LIFE
PARKS
POLITICS
RECIPES
RESTAURANTS
SAFETY
SHOPPING
SMELLS
SOUNDS
SOUVENIRS
SPORT
STORIES
TEMPLES
THOUGHTS
TOURS
USEFUL+PHRASES
TRANSPORTATION
WARNINGS
WEATHER
WILDLIFE
WORST+THING

NOTES

DAY #	DATE	WIND / RAIN / SKY	TEMP

LOCATION(S)

WHAT HAPPENED TODAY + THOUGHTS ON WHAT HAPPENED

HIGHLIGHT OF THE DAY

NOTES

DAY #	DATE	WIND / RAIN / SKY	TEMP

LOCATION(S)

WHAT HAPPENED TODAY + THOUGHTS ON WHAT HAPPENED

HIGHLIGHT OF THE DAY

NOTES

DAY #	DATE	WIND / RAIN / SKY	TEMP.

LOCATION(S)

WHAT HAPPENED TODAY + THOUGHTS ON WHAT HAPPENED

HIGHLIGHT OF THE DAY

NOTES

DAY #	DATE	WIND / RAIN / SKY	TEMP

LOCATION(S)

WHAT HAPPENED TODAY + THOUGHTS ON WHAT HAPPENED

HIGHLIGHT OF THE DAY

NOTES

DAY #	DATE	WIND / RAIN / SKY	TEMP

LOCATION(S)

WHAT HAPPENED TODAY + THOUGHTS ON WHAT HAPPENED

HIGHLIGHT OF THE DAY

NOTES

DAY #	DATE	WIND / RAIN / SKY	TEMP

LOCATION(S)

WHAT HAPPENED TODAY + THOUGHTS ON WHAT HAPPENED

HIGHLIGHT OF THE DAY

NOTES

DAY #	DATE	WIND / RAIN / SKY	TEMP

LOCATION(S)

WHAT HAPPENED TODAY + THOUGHTS ON WHAT HAPPENED

HIGHLIGHT OF THE DAY

NOTES

DAY #	DATE	WIND / RAIN / SKY	TEMP

LOCATION(S)

WHAT HAPPENED TODAY + THOUGHTS ON WHAT HAPPENED

HIGHLIGHT OF THE DAY

NOTES

DAY #	DATE	WIND / RAIN / SKY	TEMP

LOCATION(S)

WHAT HAPPENED TODAY + THOUGHTS ON WHAT HAPPENED

HIGHLIGHT OF THE DAY

NOTES

DAY #	DATE	WIND / RAIN / SKY	TEMP

LOCATION(S)

WHAT HAPPENED TODAY + THOUGHTS ON WHAT HAPPENED

HIGHLIGHT OF THE DAY

NOTES

DAY #	DATE	WIND / RAIN / SKY	TEMP

LOCATION(S)

WHAT HAPPENED TODAY + THOUGHTS ON WHAT HAPPENED

HIGHLIGHT OF THE DAY

NOTES

DAY #	DATE	WIND / RAIN / SKY	TEMP

LOCATION(S)

WHAT HAPPENED TODAY + THOUGHTS ON WHAT HAPPENED

HIGHLIGHT OF THE DAY

NOTES

DAY #	DATE	WIND / RAIN / SKY	TEMP

LOCATION(S)

WHAT HAPPENED TODAY + THOUGHTS ON WHAT HAPPENED

HIGHLIGHT OF THE DAY

NOTES

DAY #	DATE	WIND / RAIN / SKY	TEMP

LOCATION(S)

WHAT HAPPENED TODAY + THOUGHTS ON WHAT HAPPENED

HIGHLIGHT OF THE DAY

ACCOMMODATIONS
ADVENTURE
ART
AVOID+THIS
BARS
BEACHES
BELIEFS
BEST+THING
BEVERAGES
BOOKS
BOUGHT
CHURCHES
CLIMATE
CONVERSATION
CUSTOMS
DREAMS
ENCOUNTERS
EVENTS
EXHIBITIONS
EXPENSES
EXPERIENCES
FESTIVALS
FLORA+FAUNA
FOOD
GALLERIES
GARDENS
GEOGRAPHY
GETTING AROUND
HANDICRAFTS
HEALTH
HISTORY
HOLIDAYS
HOTEL
IDEAS
LANDMARKS
LANGUAGE
LEGENDS
MARKET
MEALS
MEDIA
MEMORIES
MONEY
MOVIES
MUSEUMS
MUSIC
NAMES+FACES
NATIONAL+PARKS
NATURE
NIGHT LIFE
PARKS
POLITICS
RECIPES
RESTAURANTS
SAFETY
SHOPPING
SMELLS
SOUNDS
SOUVENIRS
SPORT
STORIES
TEMPLES
THOUGHTS
TOURS
USEFUL+PHRASES
TRANSPORTATION
WARNINGS
WEATHER
WILDLIFE
WORST+THING

NOTES

DAY #	DATE	WIND / RAIN / SKY	TEMP

LOCATION(S)

WHAT HAPPENED TODAY + THOUGHTS ON WHAT HAPPENED

HIGHLIGHT OF THE DAY

NOTES

DAY #	DATE	WIND / RAIN / SKY	TEMP

LOCATION(S)

WHAT HAPPENED TODAY + THOUGHTS ON WHAT HAPPENED

HIGHLIGHT OF THE DAY

NOTES

DAY #	DATE	WIND / RAIN / SKY	TEMP

LOCATION(S)

WHAT HAPPENED TODAY + THOUGHTS ON WHAT HAPPENED

HIGHLIGHT OF THE DAY

NOTES

DEPARTURE

DEPARTED FROM	DEPARTED WHEN	DEPARTED BY

DEPARTURE NOTES

HIGHLIGHT LISTS

MOST WONDERFUL PLACES	BEST OF THE OUTDOORS	TREMENDOUS HOTELS

OUTSTANDING FOOD & BEVERAGES & DINING EXPERIENCES	GREATEST EXPERIENCES	BEST TOURS / EXPEDITIONS

D.I.Y LIST	D.I.Y LIST	D.I.Y LIST

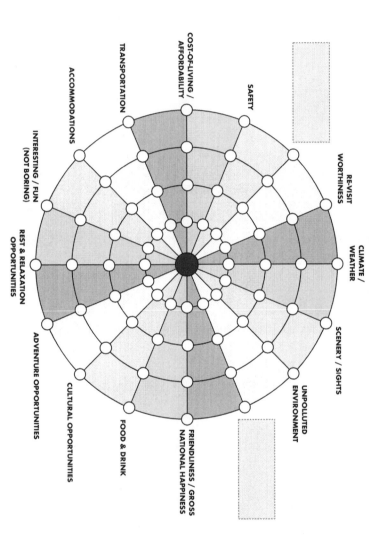

COUNTRY RADAR

- CLIMATE / WEATHER
- RE-VISIT WORTHINESS
- SAFETY
- COST-OF-LIVING / AFFORDABILITY
- TRANSPORTATION
- ACCOMMODATIONS
- INTERESTING / FUN (NOT BORING)
- REST & RELAXATION OPPORTUNITIES
- ADVENTURE OPPORTUNITIES
- CULTURAL OPPORTUNITIES
- FOOD & DRINK
- FRIENDLINESS / GROSS NATIONAL HAPPINESS
- UNPOLLUTED ENVIRONMENT
- SCENERY / SIGHTS

COUNTRY REVIEW & RATING

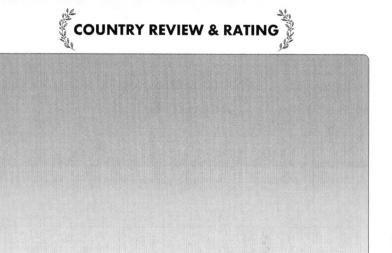

AFTERWARDS

JACK KEROUAC

LEAN FORWARD TO THE NEXT CRAZY ADVENTURE BENEATH THE SKIES

TRAVEL WISH LIST

SO . . . WHERE ELSE DO YOU WANT TO GO? WHERE + WHY + WHEN

GENERIC PACKING IDEAS

BAGGAGE
carry-on bag
duffle-bag / laundry bag
luggage
luggage locks

BATHROOM
toothbrush
toothpaste
shaving cream
sanitary products
cut-stopper
comb
brush
nail clippers
small mirror
face cloth
towel / beach towel
bar of soap
deodorant
toilet paper

BEDROOM
alarm clock / batteries
pillow
mini fan

CLOSET
suit / suit jacket
pants
shorts
under-shorts / panties
shirts / blouses
skirts
dresses
plastic hangers
swimsuit
aqua socks
rain jacket / umbrella
socks
necktie
bandana
sun hat / hat
dress shoes
walking shoes
flip-flops
belt
jacket

DESK
pens
notebook
gluestick
large envelopes
bookstand

ENTERTAINMENT
reading material
DVD

GADGETS
camera / charger
photo memory stick
batteries / charger
cellphone / charger
calculator (solar)
laptop / cords / carry
Cat5 cable
USB Thumb Drive
iPod / cords
travel speakers
headphones

HEALTH & WELLNESS
antibacterial wipes
pain killers
prescription drugs
diarrhea treatment
insect repellent
mosquito net
sunscreen
vitamins
extra pair of glasses
tweezers
thermometer
antihistamines
bandages / gauze

KITCHEN
can opener
spoon, fork, knife
plastic containers
insulated travel mug
salt n' pepper
food/snacks/drinks/water
white magic cleaner pad
slider storage bags
garbage bags

LAUNDRY ROOM
universal flat sink stopper
handy pack detergent
spot remover
clothes line

MONEY
traveller's cheques
credit cards
bank / ATM Card
security pouch
money belt
cash / various currencies

PAPERWORK
passport
visa (for country)
extra passport photos
vaccination certificates
important documents
health insurance
    information
travel tickets
personal telephone &
    address book
emergency contact list
drug prescriptions
eye prescription

REFERENCE
maps
travel guides
phrase books
travel brochures

REPAIR
safety pins
rubber bands,
cords
sewing kit
matches (waterproof
    holder)
duct tape
crazy glue

TOOLKIT
flashlight / batteries
mini screwdrivers
compass
carabineers

MEASURES & THEIR CONVERSIONS

STANDARD TO METRIC CONVERSIONS		METRIC TO STANDARD CONVERSIONS	

AREA

1 sqr inch	6.4516 sqr centimetres	1 sqr centimetre	0.155 sqr inch
1 sqr foot	0.0929 sqr metres	1 sqr meter	10.764 sqr feet
1 sqr yard	0.83613 sqr metres	1 sqr meter	1.19599 sqr yards
1 sqr acre	0.404686 sqr hectares	1 sqr hectare	0.404686 sqr hect.
1 sqr mile	2.58999 sqr kilometres	1 sqr kilometre	0.386102 sqr miles

CAPACITY

1 Canadian gallon	4.5461 litres	1 litre	0.219 Canadian gallons
1 US gallon	3.7826 litres	1 litre	0.264 US gallons

LENGTH

1 inch	2.54 centimetres	1 centimetre	0.3937 inches
1 foot	0.3048 metres	1 metre	3.2808 inches
1 yard	0.9144 metres	1 metre	1.09361 yards
1 mile	1.6093 kilometres	1 kilometre	0.6214 miles

MASS

1 gram	0.03527 ounces	1 ounce	28.349 grams
1 pound	0.4536 ounces	1 ounce	2.2046 pounds

VOLUME

1 cubic inch	16.3871 cubic centimetres	1 cubic centimetre	0.061024 cubic inch
1 cubic yard	0.76455 cubic metres	1 cubic metre	1.30795 cubic meters
1 cubic foot	0.0283 cubic metres	1 cubic metres	35.315 feet

NOTES, SKETCHES, MAPS

NOTES, SKETCHES, MAPS

NOTES, SKETCHES, MAPS

Made in the USA
San Bernardino, CA
17 August 2015